_____

PRESENTED TO

_____

FROM

_____

DATE

Starting
YOUR
Best Life
NOW

A GUIDE FOR NEW ADVENTURES
AND STAGES ON YOUR JOURNEY

JOEL OSTEEN

NEW YORK · BOSTON · NASHVILLE

All Scripture quotations, unless otherwise indicated, are taken from the *Holy Bible, New International Version®*. NIV®. Copyright © 1973, 1978, 1984 by International Bible Society. Used by permission of Zondervan Publishing House. All rights reserved.

Scriptures noted AMP are taken from Scripture quotations taken from the *Amplified® Bible*, Copyright © 1954, 1958, 1962, 1964, 1965, 1987 by The Lockman Foundation. Used by permission. (www.Lockman.org)

Scriptures noted NASB are taken from the *New American Standard Bible®*. Copyright © 1960, 1962, 1963, 1968, 1971, 1972, 1973, 1975, 1977, 1995 by the Lockman Foundation. Used by permission.

Scriptures noted NKJV are taken from the *New King James Version*. Copyright © 1979, 1980, 1982 by Thomas Nelson, Inc., Publishers.

Scriptures noted TLB are taken from *The Living Bible*, copyright © 1971. Used by permission of Tyndale House Publishers, Inc., Wheaton, Illinois 60189. All rights reserved.

Scriptures noted NLT are taken from the *Holy Bible, New Living Translation,* copyright © 1996. Used by permission of Tyndale House Publishers, Inc., Wheaton, Illinois 60189. All rights reserved.

Scriptures noted THE MESSAGE are from *The Message*. Copyright © 1993, 1994, 1995, 1996, 2000, 2001, 2002. Used by permission of NavPress Publishing Group.

Scriptures noted KJV are taken from the *King James Version* of the Bible.

Literary development and design: Koechel Peterson & Associates, Inc., Minneapolis, Minnesota.

Portions of this book have been adapted from *Your Best Life Now*, copyright © 2004 and *Daily Readings from Your Best Life Now*, copyright © 2005 by Joel Osteen. Published by FaithWords.

FaithWords
Hachette Book Group USA
237 Park Avenue, New York, NY 10169
Visit our Web site at www.faithwords.com.

The FaithWords name and logo are trademarks of Hachette Book Group, USA.

Printed in the United States of America.

First Printing: April 2007

10 9 8 7 6 5 4 3 2 1
ISBN-10: 0-446-58101-1
ISBN-13: 978-0-446-58101-1

Library of Congress Control Number: 2006936800

{CONTENTS}

INTRODUCTION

"The future is yours for the taking!" is an often quoted expression of hope passed on to graduating seniors, new employees, and wide-eyed couples on their wedding days. Yet we all know that while some people grab life with enthusiasm and take control of their futures, such a grandiose promise doesn't always pan out for everybody. Why is that?

Happy, successful, fulfilled individuals have learned how to live their best lives *now*. They make the most of the present moment and new opportunities, and thereby enhance their future. You can, too. No matter where you are or what challenges you face, you can start to enjoy your life right now.

Many people end up going through life with low self-esteem, focusing on the negative, feeling inferior or inadequate, always dwelling on reasons why they can't be happy. Others put off their happiness until some future date. Unfortunately, "someday" never comes. Today is the only day we have. We can't do anything about the past, and we don't know what the future holds. *But we can live at our full potential right now!*

In this book, you will discover just how to do that. Within these pages, you will find seven simple, yet profound, steps to start *your* best life. →

In *Starting Your Best Life Now,* we'll explore how to:

- ★ *Enlarge your vision*
- ★ *Develop a healthy self-image*
- ★ *Discover the power of your thoughts and words*
- ★ *Let go of the past*
- ★ *Find strength through adversity*
- ★ *Live to give*
- ★ *Choose to be happy.*

I CHALLENGE YOU TO BREAK OUT OF THE "BARELY-GET-BY" MENTALITY, to become the best you can be, not merely average or ordinary. To do that, you may have to rid yourself of some negative mind-sets that are holding you back and start seeing yourself as doing more, enjoying more, being more. That, my friend, is what it means to live your best life now!

ENLARGE
Your Vision

We serve the Most High God,
and His dream for your life
is so much bigger and better

than you can even imagine.

Never settle for a small view of God.
Start thinking as God thinks.

Think big.
Think increase.
Think abundance.
Think more than enough!

{ To start living your best life now, you must start looking at life through eyes of faith, visualizing the life you want to live.

DARE TO UNPACK YOUR DREAMS

From the time she was a little girl, Tara Holland dreamed of becoming Miss America. After two years as runner-up in the Miss Florida pageant, she was tempted to give up, but she chose instead to focus on her goal. She rented videos of every pageant she could find and watched them over and over again. As Tara watched each young woman crowned a winner, she pictured herself receiving the crown and walking down the runway in victory.

So when Tara was crowned Miss America in 1997, taking that long walk down the runway came as natural to her as breathing. Afterward, a reporter asked her if she was nervous about being on television, in front of millions, accepting her crown. "No," she said, "I wasn't nervous at all. You see, I had walked down that runway thousands of times before." She was simply living out the dream she had practiced so many times in her mind.

{ SO WHAT ABOUT YOU? }

What do you want to do with your life? What are your dreams? If you could write your best life story today, what would it say?

Is your first reaction to hesitate? Perhaps you most often see and describe yourself in terms of past experiences or present limitations. Perhaps you see yourself more in terms of losing or just surviving rather than fulfilling your dreams.

If you've packed away your dreams, dare to unpack them today. It's time to *enlarge your vision*. Dare to ask God to rekindle those dreams in your heart and mind. He wants to do big things and new things in your life. God wants us to be constantly increasing, to be rising to new heights. He wants to pour out "His far and beyond favor" on you (Ephesians 2:7).

Quiet your heart and receive God's Word: " 'For I know the plans I have for you,' declares the LORD, 'plans to prosper you and not to harm you, plans to give you hope and a future' " (Jeremiah 29:11).

Friend, if you will get in agreement with God, this can be the greatest time of your life. With God on your side, you cannot possibly lose. He can make a way when it looks as though there is none. He can open doors that no man can shut. He can cause you to be at the right place, at the right time. He can supernaturally turn your dreams into reality.

NEVER ALLOW YOUR OWN WRONG THINKING TO KEEP YOU FROM GOD'S BEST.

EXPECT GREAT THINGS

Centuries ago, wine was stored in leather wineskins rather than bottles. When the wineskins were new, they were soft and pliable, but as they aged, they became hardened and couldn't expand. If new wine was poured in an old wineskin, the container would burst and the wine be lost.

Interestingly, when Jesus wanted to encourage His followers to enlarge their visions, He reminded them, "You can't put new wine into old wineskins" (Matthew 9:17). He was saying that you cannot have a larger life with restricted attitudes. He is trying to do something new, but unless we're willing to change our thinking, we'll miss His opportunities for us.

God is constantly trying to plant new seeds in your heart. He's constantly trying to get you to give up antiquated ideas and spark new bursts of creativity within. He's trying to fill you with so much hope and expectancy that the seed will grow and bring forth a tremendous harvest.

Knock down the barriers and expect
God to do great things in your life.

{ ARE YOU A NEW OR OLD WINESKIN? }

Just because you're young doesn't mean your thinking hasn't already gotten old and hardened. You may have assumed that you will never be successful or do anything meaningful or enjoy the good things in life that you've seen others enjoy. You may think your life stinks and always will stink.

Will you stretch your faith and vision and get rid of those old negative mind-sets that hold you back? Start making room in your thinking for what God has in store for you. You must conceive it in your heart and mind before you can receive it. The key is to believe, to let the seeds God is placing in your life to take root so they can grow. Expect God's favor to help you break out of the ruts and rise to new heights. Expect to excel in whatever you do.

Quiet your heart and receive God's Word: "It shall be done to you according to your faith" (Matthew 9:29 NASB).

God is saying to you something similar to what the angel Gabriel told a young woman, the Virgin Mary—that she would conceive without knowing a man (Luke 1:26–38). In other words, what God wants to do in your life is not going to be by your might or power. It's going to be by His Spirit. The supernatural power of the Most High God shall come upon you and cause it to happen.

Will you believe? Remember: With God, all things are possible.

RISE TO NEW LEVELS

Todd Jacobs dreamed of starting his own computer software business, but when he got married and the first baby came along, he shelved his dreams and took a mundane job just to pay the bills. Ironically, when a terrific opportunity arose for Todd to work with one of his best friends and develop software for a well-known, established company, he turned it down. He doubted his skills and was afraid to take a chance.

Like Todd, many people miss pivotal opportunities in their lives every day because they expect nothing better. God opens new doors for them, yet regrettably they back away. Rather than launch out in faith and believe for the best, they say, "Well, that could never happen to me. That's just too good to be true."

{ DOORS OF OPPORTUNITY WILL SWING OPEN FOR YOU

God has more in store for you! His dream for your life is so much greater than you can imagine. If God showed you everything He has in store for you, it would boggle your mind.

If you have a vision for victory in your life, you can rise to a new level. But as long as your gaze is on your problems instead of on your possibilities, you risk moving in the wrong direction and missing out on the great things God wants to do in and through you.

It's a spiritual as well as a psychological fact: Your life will follow your *expectations*. If you dwell on positive thoughts, your life will move that direction; if you continually think negative thoughts, you will live a negative life, which will affect your relationship with your family and friends. If you expect defeat, failure, or mediocrity, your subconscious mind will make sure that you lose, fail, or sabotage every attempt to push above average.

WHAT YOU WILL RECEIVE IS
DIRECTLY CONNECTED TO
HOW YOU BELIEVE.

It's time to quit limiting God. God is your source, and His creativity and resources are unlimited! One idea from God can forever change the course of your life. God is not limited by what you have or don't have. God can do anything, if you will simply stop limiting Him in your thinking.

Quiet your heart and receive God's Word: "I can do all things through Him who strengthens me" (Philippians 4:13 NKJV).

When God brings opportunities across your path, step out boldly in faith, expect the best, move forward with confidence, knowing that you are well able to do what God wants you to do. Step outside that little box you've grown accustomed to. Start thinking big!

BREAK THROUGH BARRIERS

Up until the early 1950s, track-and-field experts pompously declared that no runner could break the four-minute-mile barrier. "Experts" conducted all sorts of profound studies to show that it was impossible for a human being to run that far, that fast, for that length of time. And no one ever had.

But one day a twenty-five-year-old man named Roger Bannister refused to let all those impossibilities form a stronghold in his mind. He began to train, believing he could break the record. And, sure enough, he went out and ran the "Miracle Mile," breaking the four-minute-mile barrier.

Now, here is what is so interesting about this story. Within ten years after Bannister broke the record, 336 more runners also broke it! Think of that. As far back as statisticians kept track-and-field records—hundreds of years—nobody had done it. What changed?

Simple. For all those years, the barrier was in the runners' minds. One man proved the experts wrong and hundreds ran free.

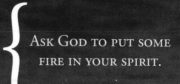

{ Ask God to put some
fire in your spirit.

{ WHAT'S HOLDING YOU BACK? }

When God led the Hebrew people out of slavery in Egypt,
the eleven-day journey to the Promised Land took forty years.
God wanted them to move forward, but they wandered in the
desert, going around the same mountain, time after time. They
were trapped in a poor, defeated mentality, focusing on their
problems, always complaining and fretting about the obstacles
between them and their destiny.

No matter what you have gone through in the past, no
matter how many setbacks you've suffered or who or what
has tried to thwart your progress, today is a new day, and
God wants to do a new thing in your life. Never let your past
determine your future.

If you will change your thinking, God can change your life. You were born to win; you were born to break through barriers; you were created to be a champion. Our God is called *El Shaddai*, "the God of more than enough." He's not "El Cheapo," the God of barely enough!

Quiet your heart and receive God's Word: "The weapons we fight with are not the weapons of the world. On the contrary, they have divine power to demolish strongholds" (2 Corinthians 10:4).

Don't accept whatever comes your way in life. Take a stand and make a difference. Your words have amazing power, so quit talking about what you can't do, and start talking about what God *can* do. Stay in an attitude of faith, and you will break through the barriers of the past.

> {
>
> Nothing is going to be able
> to keep you down.

DECLARE GOD'S FAVOR

Joseph was a young man with a heart full of dreams when his brothers sold him into slavery. Think of being hauled away to Egypt, mistreated, taken advantage of, unjustly accused of rape, and thrown into prison. But the Bible says, "The favor of God was upon Joseph" (Genesis 39:5–23). Despite overwhelming adversity, and no matter what people did to him, he continued to prosper and eventually was put in charge of all Egypt's agricultural affairs.

Ruth was a young widow providing care for her mother-in-law, Naomi, and they were practically starving during a severe famine. Yet Ruth found "favor" with the owner of the grain field (Ruth 2:10), and eventually she and Naomi's dire circumstances turned around, and their needs were supplied in abundance.

When you are living under God's "favor," or favor-minded, the Bible says, God's blessings and "love chase after me every day of my life" (Psalm 23:6 THE MESSAGE). In other words, you won't be able to outrun the good things of God. Everywhere you go, things are going to change in your favor. Every time you turn around, somebody's going to want to do something good for you.

{ ARE YOU MISSING OUT? }

The favor of God comes to us in the midst of life's challenges. In less than a year, the Old Testament character Job lost everything—his family, his business, and his health. He lived in perpetual pain. But in the midst of that dark hour, Job said to God, "You have granted me life and favor" (Job 12:10 NKJV). Amazingly, Job was not delivered, healed, and set free until chapter 42! But at the very beginning, when his circumstances appeared most helpless, Job was saying, "God, I don't care how bad the situation gets. Your favor is going to turn it around." No wonder God restored to Job twice what he had before!

Quiet your heart and receive God's Word: "Set your hope wholly and unchangeably on the grace *(divine favor)* that is coming to you" (1 Peter 1:13 AMP).

When you are going through tough times, even if your situation looks impossible, stay in an attitude of faith. Before long God's favor is going to show up, turning that difficult situation around to your benefit. Stay in an attitude of faith and declare the favor of God instead of being discouraged and developing a sour attitude. One touch of God's favor can turn everything around in your life.

NEVER GIVE UP ON GOD.

DEVELOP
a Healthy Self-Image

True self-esteem can be based

only on what God says about me—

not on what I think or feel about myself.

I am who God says I am.

{ You were made in the image of God. }

SEE YOURSELF AS GOD SEES YOU

Carly was the lone woman employed in a largely male-dominated field. She had to earn her right to be heard nearly every day. Overweight, with a halting walk from one leg being slightly shorter than the other, she heard the laughs and snide remarks made behind her back. But Carly paid little attention. She knew who she was, and she knew she was good at what she did. She walked past her detractors, receiving one promotion after another, eventually becoming the CEO of her company and a highly-sought-after expert in her field.

Carly's secret is her incredibly positive self-image. She believes that she has been made in the image of God, and that He gives her intrinsic value. She doesn't strive for the approval of others or depend on compliments to feel good about herself. Bright, friendly, articulate, and extremely competent at her work, Carly is living her best life now!

Learn to love yourself as your
heavenly Father loves you.

{ HOW DO YOU SEE YOURSELF? }

Your self-image is much like a self-portrait; it is who and what you picture yourself to be, which may or may not be an accurate reflection of who you really are. How you *feel* about yourself will have a tremendous impact on the person you become, because you will probably speak, act, and react as the person you *think* you are. The truth is, you will never rise above the image you have of yourself in your mind.

God wants us to have healthy, positive self-images, to see ourselves as champions. You may feel you're a failure, but that doesn't change God's image of you. You may feel unqualified, weak, and fearful, but God sees you as a victor! He created us in His image, and He is continually shaping us, conforming us to His character, helping us to become even more like the person He is.

Quiet your heart and receive God's Word: "My grace is sufficient for you, for my power is made perfect in weakness" (2 Corinthians 12:9).

We must learn to love ourselves, faults and all, not because we are egotists, but because that's how our heavenly Father loves us. You can walk with confidence, knowing that God loves you unconditionally. His love for you is based on what you are, not what you do. He created you as a unique individual—there has never been, nor will there ever be, another person exactly like you, and He sees you as His special masterpiece!

> Don't focus on your weaknesses;
> focus on your God.

BE STRONG AND COURAGEOUS

Perhaps you know the story. Ten of the twelve Hebrew spies sent by Moses into Canaan to check out the opposition came back and said, "It is a land flowing with milk and honey, but there are giants in the land. Moses, *we were in our own sight as grasshoppers*. They're too strong. We'll never defeat them" (Numbers 13). Compared to the giants, the mental image they had of themselves was as small helpless grasshoppers. The battle was lost before it started.

Joshua and Caleb had a totally different report. "Moses, we are well able to possess the land. Yes, there are giants there, but our God is much bigger. Because of Him, *we are well able*. Let's go in at once and possess the land." Faced with the same giants, Joshua and Caleb believed God and refused to see themselves as grasshoppers. Instead, they saw themselves as God's men, led and empowered by God.

{ DON'T BE A GRASSHOPPER }

Friend, are you allowing your weaknesses and insecurities to keep you from being your best? God already has enough "grasshoppers." He is not pleased when we mope around with a "poor me" mentality. When you do that, you're allowing your self-image to be shaped by nonbiblical concepts that are contrary to God's opinions of you. This sort of poor self-image will keep you from exercising your God-given gifts and authority, and it will rob you from experiencing the abundant life your heavenly Father wants you to have.

You and I are "well able" people. Not because we are so powerful, but because our God is so powerful. He wants you to be a "can do" person, someone who is willing, ready, and "well able" to do what He commands. When we face adversity and hardships in life, we can rise up with boldness and confidence,

knowing we can overcome them. God loves to use ordinary people just like you and me, faults and all, to do extraordinary things. If God chose to use perfect people only, He'd have no one to use.

Quiet your heart and receive God's Word: "Now thanks be to God who always leads us in triumph in Christ" (2 Corinthians 2:14 NKJV).

You can change the image you have of yourself. Start by agreeing with God. God sees you as strong and courageous, as a person of great honor and valor. Quit making excuses and start stepping out in faith, doing what God has called you to do.

KEEP GOING; KEEP GROWING. GOD HAS MUCH MORE IN STORE FOR YOU!

{ Learn to be happy with who God made you to be. }

BE AN ORIGINAL

I recall talking with Steve, a young man who suffered severe rejection as a child. His parents continually beat him down verbally, telling him he'd never amount to anything. Those destructive words crushed his self-image. Steve later discovered that his parents had hoped for a baby girl and were sorely disappointed when he was born. Sadly, Steve was convinced that he was to blame for all the heartache in his family and his parents' unhappiness.

I told him, "Steve, you cannot allow your self-esteem and your sense of value to be determined by how other people treat you. God accepts us even if everybody else rejects us." It took a while for Steve to accept the truth, but today he is well on his way to living a happy, productive life.

{ DARE TO BE HAPPY WITH WHO YOU ARE }

God doesn't want a bunch of clones. You should not let people make you feel badly about yourself because you don't fit their image of who you should be. You were created to be you. You were not created to mimic somebody else. If God had wanted you to look like a perfect model or have a different personality, He would have made you that way. When you go around trying to be like somebody else, not only does it demean you; it steals your uniqueness.

An important factor in seeing yourself God's way is to understand your intrinsic sense of value. Your sense of value cannot be based on your successes or failures, how your friends treat you, or how popular you are. It is not something we earn; indeed, we cannot earn it. God built value into us when He created us. As His unique creation, you have something to offer this world that nobody else has, that nobody else can be. Your sense of value should be based solely on the fact that you are a child of the Most High God.

Quiet your heart and receive God's Word: "We are God's workmanship" (Ephesians 2:10). The word *workmanship* implies that you are a "work in progress." God is continually shaping us into the people He wants us to be.

Be an original, not a copycat. Be secure in who God made you to be and then go out and be the best person that you can be. Even if everybody else rejects you, remember, God stands before you with His arms open wide.

IF YOU RUN THE RACE AND BE THE BEST THAT YOU CAN BE, THEN YOU CAN FEEL GOOD ABOUT YOURSELF.

BECOME WHAT
YOU BELIEVE

Perhaps at this point you are saying, "Joel, I don't want to get my hopes up. I've prayed. I've done everything I know to do. Nothing's changed. If I don't get my hopes up and nothing good happens to me, at least I won't be disappointed."

Friend, you *must* get your hopes up, or you won't have faith. Consider the fascinating account of two blind men who heard that Jesus was passing by. Despite a lifetime of blindness, they must have thought, *We don't have to stay like this. There's hope for a better future.* So they began to cry out, "Have mercy on us, Son of David!" (Matthew 9:27).

When Jesus heard their cries, He posed an intriguing question, "Do you believe that I am able to do this?" (v. 28 NASB). Jesus wanted to know whether they had genuine faith. The blind men answered, "Yes, Lord; we believe." Then the Bible says, "[Jesus] touched their eyes and said, 'Become what you believe' " (THE MESSAGE). What a powerful statement about their faith! *You will become what you believe!*

{ SO WHAT ARE YOU BELIEVING? }

Are you believing to rise above your obstacles, that you can live in health, abundance, healing, and victory? One of the most important aspects of seeing ourselves God's way involves developing a prosperous mind-set. Understand, God has already equipped you with everything you need to live a prosperous life and to fulfill your God-given destiny. He planted "seeds" inside you filled with possibilities, incredible potential, creative ideas, and dreams. But you have to start tapping into them. You've got to believe beyond a shadow of a doubt that you have what it takes.

God created you to excel, and He's given you ability, insight, talent, wisdom, and His supernatural power to do so. You don't have to figure out how God is going to solve your problems or bring it to pass. That's His responsibility. Your job is to believe.

Quiet your heart and receive God's Word: "Let the Lord be magnified, Who takes pleasure in the prosperity of His servant" (Psalm 35:27).

Start looking through eyes of faith. See yourself prospering, and keep that image in your heart and mind. You may be living in poverty at the moment, but don't ever let poverty live in you. God takes pleasure in prospering His children. As His children prosper spiritually, physically, and materially, their increase brings God pleasure.

WHAT YOU BELIEVE HAS A MUCH GREATER IMPACT ON YOUR LIFE THAN WHAT ANYBODY ELSE BELIEVES.

DISCOVER
the Power of Your
Thoughts and Words

Keep your mind set on the reality

that God is a miracle-working God.

Start talking to your mountains

about how big your God is!

{
Choose to dwell on the
promises of God's Word.

WIN THE VICTORY IN YOUR MIND

I heard a story about two farmers. When the rain fell, one farmer said, "Thank You, Lord, for watering our crops." But the other farmer said, "Yeah, but if the rain keeps up, it's going to rot the roots."

When the sun came out, the positive farmer said, "Thank You, Lord, that our crops are getting the vitamins and minerals they need. We'll have a wonderful harvest this year." But the negative farmer said, "Yeah, but if it keeps up, it's going to scorch those plants. We're never going to make a living."

{ SO WHO DO YOU SOUND LIKE? }

Whether or not you are aware of it, a war is raging all around you, and the battle is for your mind. Your enemy's number-one target is the arena of your thoughts. If he can control how you think, he'll be able to control your entire life.

Indeed, thoughts determine actions, attitudes, and self-image. Really, thoughts determine destiny, which is why the Bible warns us to guard our minds. Almost like a magnet, we draw in what we constantly think about. Whether we dwell on depressing, negative thoughts or positive, joyful thoughts, our life follows our thoughts.

And our thoughts also affect our emotions. We will feel exactly the way we think. You cannot expect to feel happy unless you think happy thoughts. Conversely, it's impossible to remain discouraged unless you first think discouraging thoughts. So much of success and failure in life begins in our minds.

To win the victory in your mind, you can't sit back passively and expect this new person to suddenly appear. If you don't think you can be successful, you never will be. When you think thoughts of mediocrity, you are destined to live an average life.

Quiet your heart and receive God's Word: "As [a man] thinks within himself, so he is" (Proverbs 23:7 NASB).

When you align your thoughts with God's thoughts and you start dwelling on the promises of His Word, when you constantly dwell on thoughts of His victory and favor, you will be propelled toward greatness, inevitably bound for increase and God's supernatural blessings. Begin by agreeing with the psalmist, "This is the day the Lord has made, and I'm going to be happy. This is going to be a great day." Magnify your God, and go out each day expecting good things.

EVERY DAY, WHEN YOU FIRST GET UP, SET YOUR MIND FOR SUCCESS.

{ God works where there is an attitude of faith. }

THINK ABOUT
YOUR THINKING

I realize that life is tough, and the demands on your life can be overwhelming. We all get knocked down occasionally and get discouraged. I am not so unrealistic as to pretend that nothing bad ever happens to us. Bad things happen to good people. Obviously, we can't ignore problems and live in denial.

But I am saying that if we get depressed or discouraged, we need not remain there. We can choose our thoughts. Nobody can make us think a certain way. If you're not happy, nobody is forcing you to be unhappy. Nobody's coercing you to be sarcastic or sullen. You decide what you will entertain in your mind.

{ WE NEED TO STOP THE EXCUSES }

We must take responsibility for our lives. As long as we keep blaming our problems on our family tree, our environment, past relationships with other people, our circumstances, and attributing blame to God, Satan, *anyone*, or *anything*, we will never be truly free and emotionally healthy. To a large extent, we can control our own destinies.

Simply because the enemy plants a negative, discouraging thought in your brain doesn't mean you have to nurture and help it grow. If you do, though, that thought will affect your emotions, your attitudes, and eventually your actions. You will be much more prone to discouragement and depression, and if you continue pondering that negative thought, it will sap the energy and strength right out of you.

So how do you ascertain the source of a thought? Easy. If it's a discouraging, destructive thought; if it brings fear, worry, doubt, or unbelief; if the thought makes you feel weak, insecure, or inadequate, I can guarantee you that thought is not from God. You need to get rid of it immediately, or it will take root and create an enemy stronghold in your mind from which attacks can be launched.

Quiet your heart and receive God's Word: "Be constantly renewed in the spirit of your mind [having a fresh mental and spiritual attitude]" (Ephesians 4:23 AMP).

It's not your circumstances that have you down; your *thoughts* about your circumstances have you down. It is possible to be in one of the biggest battles for your life and still be filled with joy and peace and victory—if you simply learn how to choose the right thoughts. Stay full of faith. Stay full of joy. Stay full of hope. If you will transform your thinking, God will transform your life.

WE CAN CHOOSE TO BELIEVE THAT GOD IS GREATER THAN OUR PROBLEMS.

{ There is a miracle in your mouth.

SPEAK TO YOUR MOUNTAINS

I love what David did when he faced the giant Goliath. He didn't complain and say, "God, why do I always have huge problems?" He didn't dwell on the fact that Goliath was a skilled warrior and he was just a shepherd boy. Rather than focus on the magnitude of the obstacle before him, David looked Goliath right in the eyes and changed his whole atmosphere through the words he spoke aloud. He said, "You come against me with sword and spear and javelin, but I come against you in the name of the LORD Almighty" (1 Samuel 17:45).

Now, those are words of faith! He didn't merely *think* them; he didn't simply *pray* them. He spoke directly to the mountain of a man in front of him and said, "Today I will give the carcasses of the Philistine army to the birds of the air" (v. 46). And with God's help, he did!

{ WHAT WOULD YOU HAVE SAID TO GOLIATH? }

Our words have tremendous power and are similar to seeds. By speaking them aloud, they are planted in our subconscious minds, take root, grow, and produce fruit of the same kind. Whether we speak positive or negative words, we will reap exactly what we sow. That's why we need to be extremely careful about what we think and say.

The Bible compares the tongue to the rudder of a huge ship (James 3:4). Although the rudder is small, it controls the ship's direction. Similarly, your tongue will control the direction of your life. You create an environment for either good or evil with your words, and you are going to have to live in that world you've created. If you're always murmuring, complaining, and talking about how bad life is, you're going to live in a pretty miserable world.

However, God wants us to use our words to *change* our negative situations. If you want to change your world, start by changing your words.

Quiet your heart and receive God's Word: "Death and life are in the power of the tongue, and those who love it will eat its fruit" (Proverbs 18:21 NASB).

The Bible clearly tells us to speak to our mountains (Mark 11:23–24). Maybe your mountain is a sickness or a troubled relationship with someone you love. Whatever your mountain is, you must speak to that obstacle. Start calling yourself healed, happy, whole, blessed, and prosperous. Stop talking to God about how big your mountains are, and start talking to your mountains about how big your God is!

GOD IS A MIRACLE-WORKING GOD.

CONFESS GOD'S WORD

In 1981, my mother was diagnosed with metastatic cancer of the liver and given just a few weeks to live. After the best doctors in the world had exhausted their efforts, they basically sent my mom home to die. However, we serve a supernatural God, and He can make a way in our lives where it looks as if there is no way.

And my mother never gave up. She refused to speak words of defeat. She found about thirty to forty favorite passages of Scripture concerning healing and walked around boldly declaring faith-filled words. As she mixed her words with God's Words, little by little, she began to feel better. She got her appetite back and slowly her strength returned. God was watching over His Word to perform it.

SPEAK WORDS OF VICTORY, HEALTH,
AND SUCCESS ABOUT YOUR LIFE.

{ HAVE YOU LISTENED TO YOUR WORDS LATELY? }

Our words are vital in bringing our dreams to pass. You have to begin speaking words of faith over your life. Your words have enormous creative power. The moment you speak something out, you give birth to it. This is a spiritual principle, and it works whether what you are saying is positive or negative.

In that regard, many times we are our own worst enemies. Statements such as, "Nothing good ever happens to me," will literally prevent you from moving ahead in life. That's why you must learn to guard your tongue and speak only faith-filled words over your life.

Understand, avoiding negative talk is not enough. You must start using your words to move forward in life. When you believe God's Word and begin to boldly confess it, mixing it with your faith, you are actually confirming that truth and making it valid in your own life. And all heaven comes to attention to back up God's Word, bringing to life the great things God has in store for you.

Quiet your heart and receive God's Word: "Reckless words pierce like a sword, but the tongue of the wise brings healing" (Proverbs 12:18).

Whether we realize it or not, our words also affect others' futures for either good or evil. We need to speak loving words of approval and acceptance, words that encourage, inspire, and motivate our family members, friends, and coworkers to reach for new heights. When we do that, we are speaking abundance and increase, declaring God's favor in their lives.

LET GO
of the Past

It's time to allow your emotional wounds to heal.

Let go of your excuses, and stop feeling
   sorry for yourself.

It's time to get rid of your victim mentality.

> If you're going to go forward in life,
> you must quit looking backward.

LET THE OLD GO

We live in a society that loves to make excuses. One person will say, "Joel, I'm a negative person because my mother was so negative." Another says, "Since my husband walked out on me, I'm always depressed." While another says, "I can't understand why I lost my wife. That's why I'm so angry."

Some people are always dwelling on their disappointments. They can't understand why their prayers aren't being answered, why their loved one wasn't healed, why they were mistreated. Some people have lived so long in self-pity that it has become part of their identity. They don't realize that God wants to restore what's been stolen.

{ ARE YOU A PRISONER OF THE PAST? }

We've all had negative things happen to us. You may have gone through things that nobody deserves to experience in life—physical, verbal, sexual, or emotional abuse. Maybe you've struggled with a chronic illness or an irreparable physical problem. Maybe your dreams don't look like they can ever work out. I don't mean to minimize those difficult experiences, but if you want to live in victory, you can't let your past poison your future.

It's time to allow emotional wounds to heal, to let go of your excuses and stop feeling sorry for yourself. It's time to get rid of your victim mentality. Nobody—not even God—ever promised that life would be fair. Quit comparing your life to someone else's, and quit dwelling on what could or should have been. Quit asking questions such as, "Why this?" or "Why that?" or "Why me?" Let go of those hurts and pains. Forgive the people who did you wrong. Forgive yourself for the mistakes you've made.

If you're not willing to let go of the old, don't expect God to do the new. If you've had some unfair things happen to you, make a decision that you're going to quit reliving those things in your memory. To constantly dwell on all the negatives and to focus on the mistakes you've made only perpetuates the problem. You will never be truly happy as long as you harbor bitterness in your heart.

Quiet your heart and receive God's Word: "Come to me, all you who are weary and burdened, and I will give you rest" (Matthew 11:28).

You may even need to forgive God. Perhaps you've been blaming Him for taking one of your loved ones. If you don't deal with it, you will wallow in self-pity. You must let go of those negative attitudes and the accompanying anger. Let it go.

TODAY CAN BE A NEW BEGINNING.

GET UP AND MOVE ON

A crippled man had spent every day for thirty-eight years lying by the pool of Bethesda, hoping for a miracle (John 5). He had a deep-seated, lingering disorder similar to what many people have today. Their maladies may not be physical; they may be emotional, but they are deep-seated, lingering disorders nonetheless. They may stem from unforgiveness or holding on to past resentments, and they affect their personality, their relationships, and their self-image.

When Jesus saw the man lying there, He asked a simple, straightforward question: "Do you want to be made well?" The man's response was interesting. He began listing all of his excuses. "I'm all alone. I don't have anyone to help me." Is it any wonder that he had not been healed?

Jesus looked at him and said, in effect, "If you are serious about getting well, get up off the ground, take up your bed, and be on your way." When the man did what Jesus told him to do, he was miraculously healed!

{ IS JESUS ASKING YOU THE SAME QUESTION? }

If you're serious about being well, you can't lie around feeling sorry for yourself. Don't waste another minute trying to figure out why certain evil things have happened to you or your loved ones. You may never know the answer. But don't use that as an excuse to wallow in self-pity. Leave it alone, get up, and move on with your life. Trust God and accept the fact that there will be some unanswered questions. Just because you don't know the answer doesn't mean that one does not exist.

Each of us should have what I call an "I Don't Understand It" file. When something comes up for which you have no reasonable answer, instead of dwelling on the "why," simply place it in this file and don't become bitter. Trust God, get up, walk out of any emotional bondage in which you have been living, and step into the great future He has for you.

Quiet your heart and receive God's Word: "Let us also lay aside every encumbrance and the sin which so easily entangles us, and let us run with endurance the race that is set before us" (Hebrews 12:1 NASB).

If you will stay in an attitude of faith and victory, God has promised that He will turn those emotional wounds around. He'll use them to your advantage, and you will come out better than you would have had they not happened to you.

WHEN YOU GO THROUGH SITUATIONS YOU DON'T
UNDERSTAND, DON'T BECOME BITTER.

FORGIVE TO BE FREE

·

The former middleweight boxing champion James "Lights Out" Toney was known to fight like a man possessed. One day, a reporter asked him why he fought with such tremendous aggression and passion. Toney replied, "It's because my dad abandoned me and my brothers and sisters when I was child, to be raised by my mother all by herself. And now I picture my dad's face on my opponent's. And I have so much hatred toward him, I just explode."

Toney let a root of bitterness get a deep hold of him, and it was poisoning his life. He was having success on the outside, but the bitterness spoiled every victory.

{ ARE YOU GETTING TO THE ROOTS? }

Many people attempt to bury the hurt and pain in their hearts or their subconscious minds. They don't realize that their bad attitudes and behaviors flow from a poisoned heart. The Bible says, "Keep thy heart with all diligence; for out of it are the issues of life" (Proverbs 4:23 KJV).

If you want to live your best life now, you must be quick to forgive. You need to forgive so you can be free and happy. When we forgive, we're not doing it just for the other person, we're doing it for our own good. When we hold on to unforgiveness and live with grudges, we are simply shutting other people out of our lives. We become isolated, alone, warped, and imprisoned by our own bitterness.

Do you realize that those walls also prevent God's blessings from pouring into your life? Those walls can stop the flow of God's favor and keep your prayers from being answered. They'll keep your dreams from coming to pass. You must forgive the people who hurt you so you can get out of prison. Get that bitterness out of your life. That's the only way you're going to truly be free.

Quiet your heart and receive God's Word: "For if you forgive men when they sin against you, your heavenly Father will also forgive you. But if you do not forgive men their sins, your Father will not forgive your sins" (Matthew 6:14–15).

You may experience genuine physical and emotional healing as you search your heart and are willing to forgive. You may see God's favor in a fresh, new way. You'll be amazed at what can happen when you release all that poison.

ONCE THE BITTER ROOT IS GONE, YOU WILL BE ABLE TO
BREAK FREE FROM YOUR PAST.

KEEP MOVING FORWARD

My dad married at a very early age, and although he went into the relationship with the best of intentions, unfortunately, the marriage failed. Daddy was heartbroken and devastated. He didn't think he'd ever preach again, much less have a family. He felt that God's blessings had lifted from his life. Dealing with his divorce was the darkest hour of his life.

But years later, Daddy told me how he had to shake himself out of his doldrums. He had to quit mourning over what he had lost and start receiving God's love. He accepted God's forgiveness and mercy, and little by little, God not only restored his ministry, He increased it as well as giving my dad a new family, too.

{ TURN YOUR SCARS INTO STARS }

Moving forward into the great future God has for you involves learning how to overcome the disappointments in your life. When you are lied to by a boss, betrayed by a friend, walked out on by a loved one, it's natural to feel remorse or sorrow. Nobody expects you to be an impenetrable rock. These kinds of losses leave indelible scars, causing you to want to hold on to your grief. It is easy to want to seek revenge.

But you must make a decision that you are going to move on. It won't happen automatically. Often, defeating disappointments and letting go of the past are the flip side of the same coin, especially when you are disappointed in yourself. When you do something wrong, don't beat yourself up about it. Admit it, seek forgiveness, and move on. Be quick to let go of your mistakes and failures, hurts, pains, and sins.

And remember that God has promised that if you will put your trust in Him to bring about the justice in your life, He will pay you back for all the unfair things that have happened to you (Isaiah 61:7–9). That means you don't have to go around trying to pay everybody back. God is your vindicator. Let Him fight your battles for you. Turn matters over to Him and let Him handle them His way (Romans 12:19).

Quiet your heart and receive God's Word: "The Lord is wonderfully good to those who wait for him, to those who seek for him" (Lamentations 3:25 TLB).

Don't live in regret or remorse or sorrow. They will only interfere with your faith. Faith must always be a present-tense reality, not a distant memory. God can turn your situation around and make it all up to you, plus much more!

YOU CAN'T UNSCRAMBLE EGGS, SO WHY TRY?

FIND STRENGTH
Through Adversity

God has a divine purpose
for every challenge
that comes into our lives.
Trials test our character
and help shape our faith.

STAND UP
ON THE INSIDE

I talked to a man the other day who had recently lost his job. He had been making a good salary working in a prestigious position, but then suddenly he was let go. I thought he would be upset and distraught. But when he came to see me, he had a big smile on his face and said, "Joel, I just lost my job, but I can't wait to see what God has in store for me next!"

He had been knocked down by circumstances outside his control, but he was still standing up on the inside.

{ HOW DETERMINED ARE YOU? }

Living your best life now is downright difficult sometimes.
Many people give up far too easily when things don't go their
way or they face adversity. Instead of persevering, they get down
and discouraged, which is understandable, especially when
they've struggled with a problem for a long time.

But we have to be more determined than that. Our circumstances in life may occasionally knock us down, but we must not stay down. Even if you can't see up on the outside, get up on the inside. Have that victor's attitude and mentality.

To live your best life now, you must act on your will, not simply your emotions. Sometimes that means you have to take steps of faith even when you are hurting, grieving, or still reeling from an attack of the enemy. It will take courage; it will definitely take determination, but you can do it if you decide to do so.

Quiet your heart and receive God's Word: "Use every piece of God's armor to resist the enemy in the time of evil, so that after the battle you will still be standing firm" (Ephesians 6:13 NLT).

Don't allow yourself to wave the white flag of surrender. Set your face like a flint and say, "God, I may not understand this, but I know You are still in control. And You said all things would work together for my good. You said You would take this evil and turn it around and use it to my advantage. So, Father, I thank You that You are going to bring me through this!" No matter what you may face in life, if you know how to get up on the inside, adversities cannot keep you down.

DEVELOP A VICTOR'S MENTALITY AND WATCH
WHAT GOD BEGINS TO DO.

> Take the pressure off your life by
> believing that God is at work.

TRUST GOD'S TIMING

Shelby was an attractive woman in her mid-thirties who genuinely desired to be married. She prayed and prayed but had never even had a serious relationship with a man. She was tempted to be discouraged, assuming she might spend her life as a single woman.

But one day she had a flat tire and pulled her car over to the side of the road. A few seconds later, another car pulled over and out stepped a handsome young man. He not only changed her tire, but he invited her out to dinner. Today they are married and wonderfully happy.

Now, think about the timing involved in their meeting. It all came down to the split second in both of their lives. This was no coincidence.

{ IS GOD LIKE AN ATM MACHINE } TO YOU?

It is our nature to want everything to be right now. When we pray for our dreams to come to pass or for an adversity to pass, we want answers immediately. But we have to understand, God has an appointed time to answer our prayers. And no matter how badly we want it sooner, it's not going to change His appointed time.

When we misunderstand God's timing, we live upset and frustrated, wondering when God is going to do something. But when you understand God's timing, you can relax, knowing that God is in control of your life and at the "appointed time" He is going to make it happen. It may be next week, next year, or ten years from now. But whenever it is, you can rest assured it will be in God's timing.

God is not like an ATM machine, where you punch in the right prayer codes and receive what you requested within twenty-four hours. No, we all have to wait and learn to trust God. The key is, are we going to wait with a good attitude and expectancy, knowing God is at work whether we can see anything happening or not?

Quiet your heart and receive God's Word: "For the vision is yet for an appointed time; but at the end it will speak, and it will not lie. Though it tarries, wait for it; because it will surely come, it will not tarry" (Habakkuk 2:3 NKJV).

We need to know that behind the scenes, God is putting all the pieces together. And one day, at the appointed time, you will see the culmination of everything that God has been doing.

GOD OFTEN WORKS THE MOST WHEN WE SEE IT
AND FEEL IT THE LEAST.

BE PATIENT

David had a big dream for his life. He had a desire to make a difference, but as a young man he spent many years as a shepherd, caring for his father's sheep. I'm sure there were plenty of times when he must have thought, *God, what am I doing here? There's no future in this place. When are You going to change this situation?* But David understood God's timing. He knew that if he would be faithful in obscurity, God would promote him at the right time. He knew God would bring his dreams to pass in due season.

You know the story. God brought David out of those fields, he defeated Goliath, and eventually he was made king of Israel.

{ ARE YOU TRYING TO FORCE DOORS OPEN? }

Perhaps you have a big dream in your heart—a dream to have a better marriage, a dream to own your own business, a dream to help hurting people—but like David, you don't really see any human way your dream could happen.

We don't always understand God's methods. His ways don't always make sense to us, but we have to realize that God sees the big picture. God isn't limited to natural, human ways of doing things. Consider this possibility: You may be ready for what God has for you, but someone in your life, who is going to be involved, is not ready yet. God has to do a work in them or another situation before your prayer can be answered according to God's will for your life. All the pieces have to come together for it to be God's perfect time.

But never fear; God is getting everything lined up in your life. You may not feel it; you may not see it. Your situation may look just as it did for the past ten years, but then one day, in a split second of time, God will bring it all together. When it is God's timing, all the forces of darkness can't stop Him. When it's your due season, God will bring it to pass.

Quiet your heart and receive God's Word: "But I trust in you, O Lord; I say, 'You are my God.' My times are in your hands" (Psalm 31:14–15).

Don't grow impatient and try to force doors to open. Don't try to make things happen in your own strength. The answer will come, and it will be right on time. He will bring your dreams to pass. Rest in Him!

LET GOD DO IT HIS WAY.

{ In the tough times we find out what we're really made of.

WALK THROUGH THE FIRE

In the Bible, we read of Job, a good man who loved God and had a heart to do what's right. Yet in a few weeks' time, he lost his business, his flocks and herds, his family, and his health. Things could not get any worse, and then his own wife told him, "Curse God and die."

But no, Job knew that God is a God of restoration. He knew God could turn any situation around. And his attitude was, *Even if I die, I'm going to die trusting God. I'm going to die believing for the best.* Sustaining faith is what got Job through those dark nights of the soul when he didn't know where to go or what to do. And, when it was all said and done, God not only turned Job's calamity around, He brought Job out with twice that he had before.

WORK WITH GOD IN THE REFINING PROCESS.

{ HOW DO YOU RESPOND TO TOUGH TIMES? }

When adversity comes knocking at the door or calamities occur, some people immediately think they have done something wrong, that God surely must be punishing them. They don't understand that God has a divine purpose for every challenge that comes into our lives. He doesn't send problems, but sometimes He allows us to go through them.

Why is that? The Bible says temptations, trials, and difficulties must come, because if we are to strengthen our spiritual muscles and grow stronger, we must have adversities to overcome and attacks to resist. Trials are intended to test our character, to test our faith. If you will learn to cooperate with God and be quick to change and correct the areas He brings to light, then you'll pass that test and be promoted to a new level.

Quiet your heart and receive God's Word: "But [God] knows the way that I take; when he has tested me, I will come forth as gold" (Job 23:10).

God often allows you to go through difficult situations to draw out those impurities in your character. You can pray and resist it, but it's not going to do any good. God is more interested in changing you than He is in changing the circumstances. You may not always like it; you may want to run from it; you may even resist it, but God is going to keep bringing up the issue again and again until you pass the test. Faith tells you the best is yet to come.

LIVE

to Give

God is a giver,

and if you want Him to pour out

His blessing and favor in your life,

then you must learn to be

a giver and not a taker.

{ God will not fill a closed fist with good things. }

BE A GIVER

I met a man not too long ago who was deeply depressed and disappointed with himself. Through a series of bad choices, he had lost his business, his family, his home, and his entire life savings. After I had prayed with him, I told him, "If you really want to be restored, you need to change your focus and go out and help somebody else in need."

He showed up at church a few weeks later, beaming with joy. He said, "Joel, I spent the last two weeks taking care of cocaine addicts, and I've never been so fulfilled. I spent my whole life living for myself, building my career, doing what I thought would bring me happiness. But now I see what really matters."

{ DO YOU SEE WHAT REALLY MATTERS? }

One of the greatest challenges we face in our quest to enjoy our best lives now is the temptation to live selfishly. Because we believe that God wants the best for us, and that He wants us to prosper, it is easy to slip into the subtle trap of selfishness. Not only will you avoid that pitfall, but you will have more joy than you dreamed possible when you live to give and not to take.

God is a giver, and He created us to be givers. The spiritual principle is that when we reach out to other people in need, God will make sure that our own needs are supplied. If you want your dreams to come to pass, help someone else fulfill his or her dreams. If you're down and discouraged, get your mind off yourself and go help meet your friend's need. Sow the seed that will bring you a harvest.

Quiet your heart and receive God's Word: "Remember the words of the Lord Jesus, how he said, It is more blessed to give than to receive" (Acts 20:35 KJV).

Perhaps you feel you have nothing to give. Sure you do! You can give a smile or a hug. You can do some menial but meaningful task to help someone. You can visit someone in the hospital or make a meal for a person who is shut in. You can write an encouraging letter. Your friend needs what you have to share. God created us to be free, but He didn't make us to function as "Lone Rangers." We need one another.

HAVE AN ATTITUDE THAT SAYS, WHO CAN I BLESS TODAY?

> Evil is never overcome
> by more evil.

WALK IN LOVE

If anybody in the Bible had a right to return evil instead of love, it was Joseph. His brothers hated him so much, they purposed to kill him but then sold him into slavery. Years went by, and Joseph experienced all sorts of troubles and heartaches. But Joseph kept a good attitude, and God continued to bless him. After thirteen years of being in prison for a crime he didn't commit, God supernaturally promoted him to the second highest position in Egypt.

When Joseph's brothers came to Egypt and suddenly found their lives were in Joseph's hands, can you imagine the fear that gripped their hearts? This was Joseph's opportunity to pay them back. Yet Joseph extended his mercy. Is it any wonder he was so blessed with God's favor? Joseph knew how to treat people right.

GOD WANTS HIS PEOPLE TO HELP
HEAL WOUNDED HEARTS.

{ CAN YOU RETURN GOOD FOR EVIL? }

How you treat other people can have a great impact on the degree of blessings and favor of God you will experience. You may have people in your life who have done you great wrong. You may feel as though your whole life has been stolen away by somebody. But if you will choose to forgive them, you can overcome that evil with good. If you do that, God will pour out His favor in your life in a fresh way. He will honor you; He will reward you, and He'll make those wrongs right.

The Bible says we are to "aim to show kindness and seek to do good" (1 Thessalonians 5:15 AMP). We must be proactive. We should be on the lookout to share His mercy, kindness, and goodness with people. Moreover, we need to be kind and do good to people even when somebody is unkind to us. The last thing they need is for you to respond angrily.

Quiet your heart and receive God's Word: "Love . . . is not touchy or fretful or resentful; it takes no account of the evil done to it [it pays no attention to a suffered wrong]" (1 Corinthians 13:5 AMP).

Keep taking the high road and be kind and courteous. Walk in love and have a good attitude. God sees what you're doing, and He is your vindicator. He will make sure your good actions and attitude will overcome that evil. If you'll keep doing the right thing, you will come out far ahead of where you would have been had you fought fire with fire.

> This world is desperate to experience the love and
> compassion of our God.

KEEP AN OPEN HEART

Are you kind and considerate to people? When that coworker walks by you and doesn't give you the time of day, are you friendly anyway? When someone speaks harshly or rudely to you, how do you respond?

Everywhere you go these days people are hurting and discouraged. They've made mistakes; their lives are in a mess. They need to feel God's compassion and His unconditional love. They don't need somebody to judge and criticize them. They need somebody to bring hope, to bring healing, to show God's mercy. Really, they are looking for a friend, somebody who will take the time to listen to their story and genuinely care.

{ WILL YOU BE A FRIEND? }

Our world is crying out for people who love unconditionally.
Certainly, when God created us, He put His supernatural love
in all of our hearts. He's placed in you the potential to have a
kind, caring, gentle, loving spirit. Created in God's image, you
have the capacity to experience God's compassion in your heart.

Jesus always took time for people. He was never too busy
with His own agenda, with His own plans. He wasn't so caught
up in Himself that He was unwilling to stop and help a person
in need. He could have easily said, "Listen, I have a schedule to
keep." But no, Jesus had compassion on people. He freely gave
of His life.

If you want to live your best life now, you must make sure
that you keep your heart of compassion open. We need to be
willing to be interrupted and inconvenienced if it means we
can help meet our friend's needs. Sometimes if we would just
take the time to listen to them, we could help initiate a healing
process in his or her life. So many people have pain bottled
up inside them. They have nobody they can talk to; they don't
trust anybody. If you can open your heart of compassion and
be that person's friend—without judging or condemning—and
simply have an ear to listen, you have the opportunity to make a
difference in that person's life.

Quiet your heart and receive God's Word: "If anyone . . . sees his brother and fellow believer in need, yet closes his heart of compassion against him, how can the love of God live and remain in him?" (1 John 3:17 AMP).

Learn to follow the flow of God's divine love. Don't ignore it. Act on it. Someone needs what you have.

Be on the lookout for people you can bless.

REAP A HARVEST

Don't let anybody convince you that it doesn't make any difference whether you give. In the Bible, a Roman named Cornelius and his family became the first recorded Gentile household to experience salvation after the resurrection of Jesus. Why was Cornelius chosen for this honor? Cornelius was told in a vision: "Your prayers and charities have not gone unnoticed by God!" (Acts 10:4 TLB). I'm not suggesting that you can buy miracles or that you have to pay God to meet your needs. But I am saying that God sees your gifts and acts of kindness. It pleases God when you give, and He will pour out His favor on you.

{ HOW MUCH SEED ARE YOU SOWING? }

All through the Bible, we find the principle of sowing and reaping. "Whatever a man sows, that he will also reap" (Galatians 6:7 NKJV). Just as a farmer must plant some seed if he hopes to reap a harvest, we, too, must plant some good seed in the fields of our families, careers, and personal relationships. If you want to reap happiness, you have to sow some "happiness" seeds by making others happy. If you want to reap financial blessing, you must sow financial seeds in the lives of others. The seed always has to lead.

God is keeping a record of every good deed you've ever done, including ones within your family. You may think it went unnoticed, but God saw it. And in your time of need, He will make sure that somebody is there to help you. Your generous gifts will come back to you. God has seen every smile you've ever given to others. He's observed every time you went out of the way to lend a helping hand. God has witnessed when you have given sacrificially, even giving money to others that perhaps you needed desperately for yourself. God has promised that your generous gifts will come back to you (see Luke 6:38).

Quiet your heart and receive God's Word: "A generous man will prosper; he who refreshes others will himself be refreshed" (Proverbs 11:25).

Here's something extra from the apostle Paul: "Each man should give what he has decided in his heart to give, not reluctantly or under compulsion, for God loves a cheerful giver. And God is able to make all grace abound to you, so that in all things at all times, having all that you need, you will abound in every good work" (2 Corinthians 9:7–8).

WHEN YOU ARE GENEROUS TO OTHERS, GOD WILL
ALWAYS BE GENEROUS WITH YOU.

CHOOSE
to Be Happy

Learn to live one day at a time.
By an act of your will, choose to
start enjoying your life right now.
Enjoy everything in your life.

{ Life is too short not to enjoy every single day. }

REJOICE IN THE LORD ALWAYS

I've heard parents say, "Well, as soon as my children get out of diapers, I'm going to be happy." Others say, "As soon as they go off to school, I'll have some free time, and I'll be happy." And some say, "Once the kids graduate, I'll start enjoying my life." Meanwhile, life passes by. "As soon as I get that promotion, as soon as I close this business deal, as soon as I retire . . ."

{ WHAT ARE YOU WAITING FOR? }

The apostle Paul wrote more than half of the New Testament while incarcerated, often in prison cells not much bigger than a small bathroom. Yet Paul wrote such amazing faith-filled words as "Rejoice in the Lord always" (Philippians 4:4 NKJV). Notice that we are to rejoice and be happy at all times. In your difficulties, when things aren't going well, make a decision to stay full of joy.

You need to understand that the enemy is out to steal your joy. The Bible says that "the joy of the Lord is your strength" (Nehemiah 8:10 NKJV), and your enemy knows if he can deceive you into living down in the dumps and depressed, then you are not going to have the necessary strength—physically, emotionally, or spiritually—to withstand his attacks.

It is a simple yet profound truth: Happiness is a choice. You don't have to wait for everything to be perfect in your life. You don't have to forgo happiness until you lose weight, break an unhealthy habit, or accomplish all your goals.

Quiet your heart and receive God's Word: "A cheerful heart is good medicine, but a crushed spirit dries up the bones" (Proverbs 17:22).

Choose to be happy and enjoy your life! When you do that, not only will you feel better, but your faith will cause God to show up and work wonders. To do so, you must learn to live one day at a time; better yet, make the most of this moment. It's good to set goals, but if you're always living in the future, you're never really enjoying the present in the way God wants you to.

By an act of your will, choose to start enjoying your life right now. Enjoy your family, friends, and health; enjoy everything in your life. Happiness is a decision you make, not an emotion you feel.

LEARN HOW TO SMILE AND LAUGH. QUIT BEING SO UPTIGHT AND STRESSED OUT.

{ Subtle compromises of excellence will keep you from God's best. }

EXCEL IN
INTEGRITY

I heard about a guy who left early from work one day to go to his grandmother's funeral. The next morning at work, his boss came up and said, "Do you believe in life after death?"

The employee looked puzzled and finally said, "Well, yes; I do."

The boss said, "Boy, that makes me feel a whole lot better."

"Why? What are you talking about?"

The boss said, "Well, yesterday after you left to attend your grandmother's funeral, she stopped by to visit you."

{ ARE YOU WILLING TO PAY THE PRICE TO DO THE RIGHT THING? }

For many people, mediocrity is the norm; they want to do as little as they possibly can and still get by. But God has called us to be people of excellence and integrity. A person of integrity is open and honest and true to his word. He or she doesn't have any hidden agendas or ulterior motives. People of integrity are the same in private as they are in public. They do what's right whether anybody is watching or not.

People of excellence give their employers a full day's work; they don't come in late, leave early, or call in sick when they are not. When you have an excellent spirit, it shows up in the quality of your homework, and the attitude with which you do it.

If you don't have integrity, you will never reach your highest potential. Integrity is the foundation on which a truly successful life is built. Every time you compromise, every time you are less than honest, you are causing a slight crack in the foundation. If you continue compromising, that foundation will never be able to hold what God wants to build. You'll never have lasting prosperity if you don't first have integrity.

Quiet your heart and receive God's Word: "Whoever can be trusted with very little can also be trusted with much, and whoever is dishonest with very little will also be dishonest with much" (Luke 16:10).

God's people are people of excellence. Remember: You represent Almighty God. How you live, how you care for your family and do your work, is all a reflection on our God. If you want to live your best life now, whatever you do, give your best effort and do it as if you are doing it for God. If you'll work with that standard in mind, God promises to reward you, and others will be attracted to our God.

START AIMING FOR EXCELLENCE IN EVERYTHING YOU DO.

{

Stay passionate about seeing your
dreams come to pass.

ENJOY YOUR BEST
LIFE NOW

For several years, I noticed Jackie sitting down front at
Lakewood Church. Week after week, she participated with
tremendous enthusiasm, singing with all her heart, radiating
joy. I didn't know who she was, but when I'd bring the message,
Jackie would smile and nod her head, as though she was
encouraging me, "Come on, Joel. Tell me more."

When a staff position become available in our Women's
Ministry, the first thing I said was, "Somebody go find that lady
who sits down front. There's nobody I'd rather have represent
us than somebody like her!" We hired her, and she continues to
inspire and encourage people.

{ ARE YOU ON FIRE? }

God's people should be the happiest people on earth! So happy, in fact, that other people notice. Living your best life now is living with enthusiasm and being excited about the life God has given you. It is believing for more good things in the days ahead, but it is also living in the moment and enjoying it to the hilt!

One of the main reasons we lose our enthusiasm in life is because we start to take for granted what God has done for us as well as His greatest gift of all to us—Himself! Don't allow your relationship with Him to become stale or your appreciation for His goodness to become common. Our lives need to be inspired, infused, filled afresh with His goodness every day.

Make a decision that you are not going to live another day without the joy of the Lord in your life; without love, peace, and passion; without being excited about your life. And understand that you don't have to have something extraordinary happening in your life to be excited. You may not have the perfect job or the perfect marriage, but you can still choose to live each day aglow with God's presence.

Quiet your heart and receive God's Word: "Never lag in zeal and in earnest endeavor; be aglow and burning with the Spirit, serving the Lord" (Romans 12:11 AMP).

DON'T JUST GO THROUGH THE MOTIONS IN LIFE.
HAVE SOME ENTHUSIASM.

If you want to see God's favor, do everything with your whole heart. Do it with passion and some fire. Not only will you feel better, but that fire will spread, and soon other people will want what you have. Wherever you are in life, make the most of it and be the best you can be. God will take you places you've never dreamed of, and you will be having your best life now.